PowerKids Readers:
Nature Books™

Apples

Kristin Ward

The Rosen Publishing Group's
PowerKids Press™
New York

For Thomas and Mak, with love

Published in 2000 by The Rosen Publishing Group, Inc.
29 East 21st Street, New York, NY 10010

Copyright © 2000 by The Rosen Publishing Group, Inc.

First Edition

Book design: Michael de Guzman

Photo Credits: p.1 © 1995 PhotoDisc; p. 5 CORBIS/Kevin R. Morris; p. 7 © Margaret Walton/International Stock; p. 9 © Edgar Webber/FPG International; p. 11 © Bob Firth/International Stock; p. 13 CORBIS/Mark Gibson; pp. 15, 19, 21 by Suzanne Mapes; p. 17 CORBIS/Dewitt Jones.

Ward, Kristin.
     Apples / by Kristin Ward.
       p. cm. — (Nature books)
     Includes index.
     Summary: Describes what apples look like, how they grow, and what we use them for.
     ISBN 0-8239-5528-1 (library binding)
     1. Apples—Harvesting—Juvenile literature. [1. Apples—Harvesting.] I. Title.
II. Series: Nature books (New York, N.Y.)
     SB363.35.W27   1999
     634'.115—DC21   98-52680
                                                              CIP
                                                              AC

Manufactured in the United States of America

Contents

Apples grow on trees.

Apples can be red, yellow, or green.

7

Apples grow in the spring. They start out as buds. They will grow and grow.

In the fall, apples are
ready to be picked.

It is fun to pick apples.
You can pull apples right
off the branch.

There are lots of apples on the branches. Apple pickers need big baskets.

15

Apples can be used to make juice.

Apples can be used to make pies.

Sometimes apples taste great just as they are.

Words to Know

 APPLE

 BASKET

 BRANCH

 BUD

 JUICE

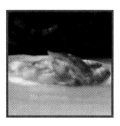 PIE

Here are more books to read about apples:
Apple Picking Time
by Michele Benoit Slawson, illustrated by
Deborah Kogan Ray
Dragonfly

Apple Trees (Early Bird Nature Books)
by Dorothy Hinshaw Patent, photographs by
William Munoz
Lerner Publications

To learn more about apples, check out these
Web sites:
http://orchard.uvm.edu/
http://www.tcgcs.com/~nrolls/garden.html

Index

Word Count: 84

Note to Librarians, Teachers, and Parents

PowerKids Readers (Nature Books) are specially designed to help emergent and beginning readers build their skills in reading for information. Simple vocabulary and concepts are paired with photographs of real kids in real-life situations or stunning, detailed images from the natural world around them. Readers will respond to written language by linking meaning with their own everyday experiences and observations. Sentences are short and simple, employing a basic vocabulary of sight words, as well as new words that describe objects or processes that take place in the natural world. Large type, clean design, and photographs corresponding directly to the text all help children to decipher meaning. Features such as a contents page, picture glossary, and index help children get the most out of PowerKids Readers. They also introduce children to the basic elements of a book, which they will encounter in their future reading experiences. Lists of related books and Web sites encourage kids to explore other sources and to continue the process of learning.